Lucas and Emily's Dog Adventure

Written by
Dave Grunenwald

Illustrated by
Bonnie Lemaire

Halo
PUBLISHING
INTERNATIONAL

Halo Publishing International
7550 WIH-10 #800, PMB 2069,
San Antonio, TX 78229

First Edition, June 2024
ISBN: 978-1-63765-596-2
Library of Congress Control Number: 2024906583

Halo Publishing International is a self-publishing company that publishes adult fiction and non-fiction, children's literature, self-help, spiritual, and faith-based books. Do you have a book idea you would like us to consider publishing? Please visit www.halopublishing.com for more information.

This book is dedicated to grandparents and grandchildren, around the world, who enjoy their pets, especially dogs, and sharing their own adventures with others.

Continued thanks for their assistance goes to my daughters Jill Grunenwald and Amy Burke, and to my associate, Terry Stephens.

Special thanks to the creativity of Kelly New; her husband, Zach; and father, Kurt Kalina.

"Let's go for a stroll," Grandma says to Lucas. "Grandpa went golfing with friends today, and we can spend some time together."

"That's a great idea," he answers as they head out the front door.

"Good morning," yells Carol, Grandma's friend across the street. "Eva, Eliot, and I are heading to the Metropark to walk our dogs Parker and Riley. Do you want to join us?"

"Yes!" shouts Lucas. "Emily is on her way over, and she can join us."

"That's great," says Carol, Eva and Eliot's grandmother, whom they call Gigi. "We usually do this once a month and always on Wednesday."

They all head to the Metropark, which is just a short distance away, as Emily joins them.

6

"We really like strolling through the Metropark," says Lucas. "Just recently, we had a great day there while we fished in the pond and flew a kite together."

The kids are all excited as they continue their adventure.

As they walk, Eliot seems a bit quiet, so Gigi asks, "Eliot, are you excited to walk Parker and Riley in the park?"

"I like the park, but the geese are scary!" says Eliot.

Eva is seven, and Eliot is two, so she knows he has only walked with the dogs in the Metropark a few times. He is still getting used to the surroundings.

"Hmmm," murmurs Gigi as she thinks to herself. "You know, Eliot, the geese are just trying to protect their babies."

7

8

It is a beautiful, warm day; the sun shines brightly. There is not a cloud in the sky. Soon, they make their way towards the entrance to the Metropark.

"We love it here," Eva shouts.

Eliot holds Riley's leash, and Eva holds Parker's, the bigger of the two dogs. Lucas and Emily pet the dogs as they all walk.

"We are lucky to have such a beautiful Metropark nearby," says Lucas as they enter the park, scatter, and head to the playground.

"I'm going up on the slide," Eva says as she makes her way towards the playground.

The kids hand the leashes to Gigi and Grandma. They take turns on the slides and swings, laughing and talking as they play.

Parker and Riley are getting lots of attention as other kids come over to pet them.

"What are their names?" one little boy asks.

"Parker and Riley," Gigi says as some of the other boys and girls join them. "They both love kids!" she adds.

"Geez," says Eliot, coming to join Gigi, "the kids love the dogs." He is somewhat surprised.

Soon, Lucas, Emily, Eva, and Eliot are around the dogs, along with the other kids. They are all having fun.

"The dogs—especially Parker—really like kids," says Gigi as the children surround the dogs and pet them.

The kids see how easily the dogs can make friends.

"Sometimes it is hard to make new friends," says Grandma, "but Parker and Riley seem good at it."

Thinking back to Eliot's comment about the geese, Gigi says, "Dogs are naturals at making new friends. They live in the moment."

"Like many pets, Parker and Riley help us feel loved and protected," Gigi says to Eliot and Eva.

"We have pets too," says Lucas. "Emily has a dog named Fred, and I have two cats, Miko and Allie."

"I love Fred," says Emily. "He is part of our family."

"Miko and Allie are the best," says Lucas. "They are very friendly and make me feel good. I love when they purr," he adds as he imitates them.

"You see, Eliot, our pets make us feel good about ourselves and the friends we meet," says Gigi. "They like us just the way we are."

"Let's take a walk down the path over there," says Grandma, pointing.

"What a neat idea!" some of them can be heard saying as they head towards the pond, which is where the path begins.

As they walk down the path, Gigi points out the different flowers.

"That is a daisy, and beyond is a bed of hydrangea," she says. "There are many different kinds of flowers, trees, and bushes here."

"Look over there," says Grandma, pointing to the signs along the path. "Those signs give us information about the nature we are surrounded by."

Eliot realizes he enjoys being here; it makes him happy.

As they get closer, the kids spot the pond.

"I caught my first fish here," shouts Emily. "What fun we had that day."

"We'll come fishing with Grandpa someday soon," says Grandma. "Eva and Eliot, would you like to join us?" she asks.

"Of course!" they happily respond.

After a fun walk on the path and around the pond, they all walk towards the exit as they begin to head home.

As the kids make their way towards the park's exit, Eliot spots the geese. They are large and grey, as well as black and white. There are about thirty of them. He braces for action, wearing a frown on his face.

Parker and Riley, barking, run towards the geese that do not seem to mind the dogs' presence.

"Do the dogs like the geese?" Eliot asks Gigi.

"They do," she responds. "Remember, our pets make us feel safe and comfortable. You can explore with them, knowing they are good friends, but also great protectors."

She adds, "In this case, they show us that the geese are nothing to be afraid of."

The geese spread out as they walk slowly near the path to the exit. They do not seem to be going anywhere in particular while they look for food.

Eliot decides to approach the geese.

As he walks closer, Gigi hands him Parker's leash so he can walk with, as Gigi put it, "his protector." Eliot becomes braver as he approaches the geese.

Parker begins to bark, and the geese look their way and simply watch. Some amble towards Eliot and Parker as they get nearer.

"Remember, they are just animals," says Gigi. "Parker likes them, so you should like them too!"

"Hi, geese, I am Eliot. How are you?"

Gigi beams with pride as Eliot begins to conquer his fear.

Eliot and Parker make their way through the geese, as the geese move slowly to get out of the way.

"Wow, lots of geese, " says Eliot.

As they walk, Parker barks, and the geese flap their wings.

"This is great," says Lucas as he, Emily, and Eva join Eliot.

"I've never seen so many geese," says Emily.

They all begin to count. "One...two...three..."

"How do you feel about the geese now, Eliot?" Gigi asks him.

"They are nice," he answers. "Parker likes them, so I can too!"

"I am proud of you, Eliot, for facing your fear," says Gigi.

The kids continue to pet the dogs and wander through the geese.

"This is a day I will remember forever," says Eva.

The kids enjoy themselves as the sun begins to set.

As they make their way home, Eliot asks, "Why do dogs like everyone?"

"Dogs are friendly until there is a reason not to be. Just like the geese, they protect each other. They are like you and me," Gigi says. "They can teach us a lot about ourselves and others."

"Do they ever get mad?" he asks.

"If Parker sees someone treating you meanly, or if he is treated meanly by another person or animal, he might growl. He just wants you to be safe," she says.

They pass the homes of lots of friends as they make their way down the street, waving as they see people they know.

On the way home, Eliot is holding Parker's leash, and Eva is holding Riley's leash, the opposite of how they walked earlier.

"I can learn a lot from Parker," says Eliot.

"Dogs can teach us a lot of things—for example, how to love unconditionally," Gigi answers. "They also can teach us how to forgive and how to be loyal."

"Wow," Emily says, "I didn't know dogs were such great teachers!"

"Thanks for inviting us," says Grandma as they arrive at Gigi's house.

"Yes, thank you," Lucas says. "We had a great time."

"I learned a lot today about dogs and other animals," says Eliot. "Parker taught me I'm not so afraid of some things anymore."

They all say goodbye as they part company.

"Grandpa!" Lucas shouts as they get home. "We missed you."

"I missed you too," says Grandpa.

"We went for a walk in the park with Gigi and her grandkids, along with their dogs Parker and Riley."

"Sounds like a good day," Grandpa says.

"Is playing with dogs a merit badge, Grandpa?" asks Lucas.

"Yes. In fact, there is a special book just for dog lovers. Perhaps, someday, we will plan a day with all of our pets!" Grandpa says.

To be continued...

For more information, visit
www.grandparentmeritbadges.com,
its related blog, and its Facebook page.
As we like to say:

DISCONNECT FROM THE DIGITAL™
AND
RECONNECT WITH THOSE WHO MATTER MOST

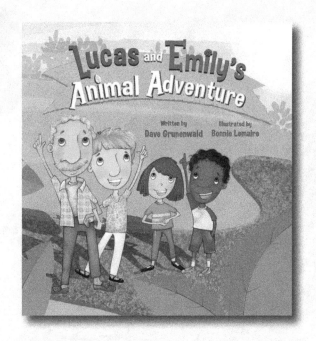

Lucas and Emily's Animal Adventure

"Lucas and Emily's Animal Adventure" is based on the Grandparent Merit Badges™, a series of kits, which launched in 2021. The kits are designed to encourage grandparents and grandkids to disconnect from the digital world and to spend more time together doing simple but fun activities. The adventure books are designed to be a series of stories about family members spending time and having fun doing things together.

ISBN Hardcover: 978-1-63765-413-2
ISBN Paperback: 978-1-63765-414-9

Lucas and Emily's Outdoor Adventure

"Lucas and Emily's Outdoor Adventure" is based on the Grandparent Merit Badges™, a series of kits that launched in 2021. The kits are designed to encourage grandparents and grandkids to disconnect from the digital world and to spend more time together doing simple but fun activities. The adventure books are designed to be a series of stories about family members spending time and having fun doing things together.

ISBN Hardcover: 978-1-63765-497-2
ISBN Paperback: 978-1-63765-498-9

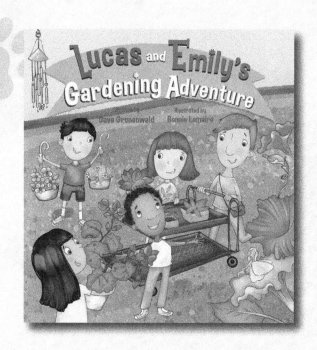

Lucas and Emily's Gardening Adventure

"Lucas and Emily's Gardening Adventure" is based on the Grandparent Merit Badges™, a series of kits that launched in 2021. The kits are designed to encourage grandparents, grandkids, and any type of family members or friends, to disconnect from the digital world and to spend more time together doing simple, but fun activities. The adventure books are designed to be a series of stories about family members and friends spending time and having fun doing things together.

ISBN Hardcover: 978-1-63765-554-2
ISBN Paperback: 978-1-63765-555-9

Printed in the USA
CPSIA information can be obtained
at www.ICGtesting.com
CBHW060400300724
12357CB00005BA/9